THE LAST-MINUTE COOKBOOK

Quick Meals for Busy People

by Jane Kobayashi

W.W. Norton & Company
New York   London

Copyright ©1994 by Becker & Mayer Ltd.

First Edition
All rights reserved
Printed in the United States of America

The text of this book is composed in Futura Bold and Garamond 3 with the display set in Garamond 3 (extended).

Manufacturing by MC USA

Book design and composition by Jane Kobayashi

ISBN 0-393-31151-1

W. W. Norton & Company, Inc., 500 Fifth Avenue, New York, N.Y. 10110
W. W. Norton & Company Ltd., 10 Coptic Street, London WC1A 1PU

1 2 3 4 5 6 7 8 9 0

A little note:

A majority of the main dishes can be made in 30 minutes. Here are some additional hints to save more time.

- Use precrushed garlic and ginger. These can be found in small jars in the produce section.

- Use prewashed and prepared produce when possible (lettuce, spinach, etc.).

- Use pregrated cheeses.

- Where chicken stock is needed, I've suggested using 14½-oz. cans for convenience. Feel free to substitute bouillon or homemade stock.

Add Your Own Recipes
In the back of this book you'll find several blank pages to add your own recipes and shopping lists, so you can remember the ingredients to all *your* favorite dishes.

So the next time you're stuck in the grocery store, suffering from "recipe block," pick one of my recipes or choose one of your own.

RECIPE INDEX

APPETIZERS & STARTERS

Beef Skewers & Spicy Sesame Sauce	8–9
Tricolor Roasted Peppers	10–11
Olive Crostini Toasts	12–13
Cheese & Herb Puff Pastry Squares	14–15

SOUPS hot & cold

Yucatan Lime & Tortilla Soup	18–19
Fresh Garden Gazpacho	20–21
Carrot Ginger Soup	22–23
Potato, Leek & Corn Soup	24–25

SALADS

Warm Spinach Salad & Baked Goat Cheese	28–29
Classic Caesar Salad	30–31
Orange-Almond Salad with Sesame Vinaigrette	32–33
Fresh Tomatoes, Farfalle & Feta Salad	34–35

MAIN DISHES

Poultry

Stir-Fried Chicken with Broccoli & Cashews	38–39
Fresh Rosemary Chicken with Walnuts	40–41
Shredded Chicken Tacos	42–43
Grilled Salad with Goat Cheese Filled Chicken	44–45
Parsley, Sage, Rosemary & Thyme Chicken	46–47

Meat

Sesame Flank Steak	48–49
Beef with Asparagus	50–51
Colorful Teriyaki Kebabs	52–53
Mustard Pork Chops with Couscous	54–55

Seafood

Grilled Halibut with Basil–Pine Nut Butter	56–57
Salmon, Fresh Tomatoes & Spaghettini	58–59
Quick Garlic Shrimp	60–61
Basil & Lemon Stuffed Trout	62–63
Spicy Thai Swordfish	64–65

Pasta

Agnolotti, Zucchini, & Herbs	66–67
Cheese Ravioli with Roasted Red Pepper Sauce	68–69
Penne à la Puttanesca	70–71
Pesto Linguine	72–73

SIMPLY DELICIOUS DESSERTS

Ice Cream Filled Puff Pastry & Raspberry Sauce	76–77
Apple Blackberry Walnut Cobbler	78–79
Triple Chocolate Walnut Brownies	80–81
Poached Pears with Maple Pecan Sauce	82–83

FAVORITE RECIPE INGREDIENT LISTS   85–96

APPETIZERS & STARTERS

Appetizers & Starters

BEEF SKEWERS & SPICY SESAME SAUCE
Yields 4 servings

your preparation time: *15 minutes*

total time until ready: *20 minutes*

---

1. Preheat grill or broiler.
2. *Skewers:* Cut **1 lb. boneless sirloin steak** into 1" strips. Skewer each strip lengthwise on **6" bamboo skewers**.
3. *Marinade.* Combine **½ C. light soy sauce, 1 T. honey, 2 T. sesame oil, 1 t. grated fresh gingerroot (or 1 t. precrushed)** and **½ t. crushed red pepper flakes**. Pour over meat. Coat all sides and marinate unrefrigerated while you make sauce.
4. *Sesame sauce:* In a small saucepan, heat **1 t. sesame oil. Add 2 minced or pressed garlic cloves (or 1 t. precrushed)** and **1 finely chopped green onion stalk**. Sauté until soft. Add **1 C. chicken stock, ¼ C. light soy sauce, 2 T. toasted sesame seeds** and **½ t. crushed red pepper flakes**. Keep warm while meat is being prepared.
5. Grill or broil the skewers until medium-rare (30–40 seconds per side).
6. Serve the skewers with the dipping sauce.

Beef Skewers & Spicy Sesame Sauce

SHOPPING LIST

PRODUCE	fresh gingerroot (1 small piece, or 1 t. precrushed)
	garlic (2 cloves, or 1 t. precrushed)
	green onion (1 stalk)
MEAT/FISH	boneless sirloin steak (1 lb.)
CANNED ITEMS	chicken stock (1 C. or half a 14 1/2-oz. can)
SEASONINGS	crushed red pepper flakes (1 t.)
SPECIALTY/ ETHNIC ITEMS	light soy sauce (3/4 C.)
	sesame oil (2 T. + 1 t.)
	toasted sesame seeds (2 T.)
MISC. ITEMS	6" bamboo skewers (1 package)
	honey (1 T.)

Appetizers & Starters

TRICOLOR ROASTED PEPPERS
Yields 4 servings

your preparation time: *20 minutes*

total time until ready: *25–30 minutes*

---

1. Preheat the broiler. Place **3 bell peppers (1 red, 1 yellow and 1 green)** on a cookie sheet and grill on all sides until the skin is blackened.
2. While peppers are roasting, *make the dressing:* in a small glass bowl, combine **1/4 C. extra virgin olive oil, 4 T. balsamic vinegar, 1 minced or pressed garlic clove (or 1/2 t. precrushed)** and **salt and pepper to taste**.
3. Place charred peppers in a plastic bag to sweat for 5 minutes. Peel off skin and discard stems and seeds. Slice the peppers into thin strips lengthwise.
4. Arrange pepper strips on a plate. Spoon the dressing over the peppers. Sprinkle **10 chopped fresh basil leaves (or 1/2 T. dried basil)** on top of peppers. Add **freshly ground black pepper to taste**.
5. Serve with **goat cheese or fresh buffalo mozzarella sliced in rounds** and **French baguette slices**.

SHOPPING LIST

PRODUCE	red bell pepper (1 medium)
	yellow bell pepper (1 medium)
	green bell pepper (1 medium)
	garlic (1 clove, or 1/2 t. precrushed)
	fresh basil (10 leaves)*
DAIRY	fresh buffalo mozzarella (1/4 lb.)
	or goat cheese (6-oz. log)
SEASONINGS	salt and pepper (to taste)
MISC. ITEMS	extra virgin olive oil (1/4 C.)
	balsamic vinegar (4 T.)
	French baguette

If not available substitute dried basil (1/2 T.)

OLIVE CROSTINI TOASTS

Yields 4-6 servings

your preparation time: *15 minutes*

total time until ready: *20 minutes*

---

1. Preheat broiler.
2. Chop **½ C. (4½-oz. can) black olives** and **½ C. (3-oz. jar) green olives with pimientos** in a food processor. Transfer to a medium bowl.
3. Drop **2 garlic cloves, ½ C. grated Parmesan cheese, 4 T. butter** and **2 T. olive oil** into the food processor and mix it into a paste.
4. Add mixture to the olives.
5. Add **½ C. grated Monterey Jack cheese** and **¼ C. chopped fresh parsley** and mix well.
6. Cut a **French baguette** into thin slices. Spread slices with olive mixture.
7. Cook under broiler until golden and bubbly.

Olive Crostini Toasts

SHOPPING LIST

PRODUCE	garlic (2 cloves)
	parsley (1 bunch)
DAIRY	butter (4 T. or 1/2 stick)
	grated Parmesan cheese (1/2 C.)
	grated Monterey Jack cheese (1/2 C. or 2 oz.)
CANNED ITEMS	chopped black olives (1/2 C. or 4 1/2-oz. can)
	green olives with pimientos (1/2 C. or 3-oz. jar)
MISC. ITEMS	olive oil (2 T.)
	French baguette

Appetizers & Starters

CHEESE & HERB PUFF PASTRY SQUARES
Yields 4 servings

your preparation time: *10 minutes*

total time until ready: *25–30 minutes*

---

1. Preheat oven to 375°.
2. Take **1 Pepperidge Farm Frozen Puff Pastry Sheet** and roll it until it is a rectangle, double in size.
3. Lay the dough on a cookie sheet lined with parchment or wax paper. Brush the dough with **olive oil.**
4. Sprinkle half the dough with your favorite cheese and herb combinations (for example):
    gorgonzola cheese and basil
    goat cheese, chopped olives and thyme
    cheddar cheese, sour cream and pimientos
    Monterey Jack cheese, diced tomatoes and salsa
    mozzarella, sundried tomatoes and basil
5. Fold the other half of the dough on top of fillings.
6. Brush the top with **milk** and bake in oven until golden brown (15–20 minutes).
7. Cut into squares and serve hot.

Cheese & Herb Puff Pastry Squares

SHOPPING LIST

PRODUCE	choose fillings (see examples)
DAIRY	milk (to brush on dough) choose fillings (see examples)
CANNED ITEMS	choose fillings (see examples)
SEASONINGS	choose seasonings (see examples)
FROZEN ITEMS	Pepperidge Farm Frozen Puff Pastry Sheets (A 17¼-oz. package contains 2 unbaked sheets.)
MISC. ITEMS	olive oil (to brush on dough) parchment or wax paper (to line cookie sheet)

SOUPS
HOT & COLD

YUCATAN LIME & TORTILLA SOUP

Yields 4 servings

your preparation time: 5 minutes

total time until ready: 25–30 minutes

This is a very simple recipe. Most of the time required is for simmering the tomatoes.

1. In a medium saucepan, sauté **½ chopped onion** and **1 minced or pressed garlic clove (or ½ t. precrushed)** in **2 T. olive oil** until tender.
2. Add **1–2 seeded and minced serrano chilies, 1 t. ground cumin** and **½ t. dried oregano.** Sauté for 1 minute. Add **4 C. chopped fresh tomatoes** and simmer, stirring occasionally, for 5 minutes.
3. Add **three 14½-oz. cans of chicken stock** and simmer for 15 minutes.
4. While soup is simmering, cut **4–6 corn tortillas** into ¼" strips and fry them *very quickly* in *very* hot oil. Drain on paper towels.
5. Add **⅓ C. fresh-squeezed lime juice** to the soup. **Salt and pepper to taste.**
6. Serve hot, topped with **grated Monterey Jack cheese** and fried tortillas.

Yucatan Lime & Tortilla Soup

SHOPPING LIST

PRODUCE	onion (1/2 medium)
	garlic (1 clove, or 1/2 t. precrushed)
	serrano chilies (1–2)
	tomatoes (4–6 medium-large)
	limes (3–4)
DAIRY	grated Monterey Jack cheese (for topping)
CANNED ITEMS	chicken stock (three 14 1/2-oz. cans)
SEASONINGS	ground cumin (1 t.)
	dried oregano (1/2 t.)
	salt and pepper (to taste)
SPECIALTY/ ETHNIC ITEMS	corn tortillas (4–6)*
MISC. ITEMS	olive oil (2 T.)
	vegetable oil (for frying tortillas)

To save time, store-bought unsalted tortilla chips can be used.

Soups

FRESH GARDEN GAZPACHO
Yields 6 servings

your preparation time: *10–15 minutes*

total time until ready: *10–15 minutes*

---

1. In a large glass bowl, combine the following ingredients: **3–4 very ripe tomatoes cut into quarters, 1 peeled, sliced medium cucumber, 1 cored, seeded and sliced red bell pepper, 1 chopped celery stalk, 1 seeded and minced green serrano chili, 1 chopped green onion stalk, 3 T. tomato paste, 1 t. salt, 1/4 t. pepper, 1/4 t. cayenne pepper, 4 T. olive oil, 2 dashes of Worcestershire sauce** and **2 T. balsamic or white wine vinegar**.
2. In batches, process the ingredients in a food processor fitted with a steel blade until minced.
3. Return to the bowl and add an **11 1/2-oz. can of tomato juice** and the **juice of 1 lime.**
4. Serve immediately or cover and chill. Serve with **lemon wedges, croutons,** and **a dollop of sour cream** or **plain nonfat yogurt.**

Fresh Garden Gazpacho

SHOPPING LIST

PRODUCE	very ripe tomatoes (3–4 medium)
	cucumber (1 medium)
	red bell pepper (1 medium)
	celery stalk (1 medium)
	green serrano chili (1 medium)
	green onion (1 stalk)
	lime (1)
	lemon (1) for garnish (optional)
DAIRY	sour cream or plain nonfat yogurt (8-oz. carton) for garnish (optional)
CANNED ITEMS	tomato paste (3 T.)
	tomato juice (11 1/2-oz. can)
SEASONINGS	salt (1 t.)
	pepper (1/4 t.)
	cayenne pepper (1/4 t.)
	Worcestershire sauce (2 dashes)
MISC. ITEMS	olive oil (4 T.)
	balsamic or white wine vinegar (2 T.)
	croutons for garnish (optional)

CARROT GINGER SOUP

Yields 4-6 servings

your preparation time: *5 minutes*

total time until ready: *30 minutes*

This is a very simple recipe. Most of the time required is for simmering the carrots.

1. In a large saucepan, melt **3 T. unsalted butter** over medium heat. Add **½ chopped onion, 2 T. grated fresh gingerroot (or 2 T. precrushed)** and **1 minced or pressed garlic clove (or ½ t. precrushed)** and sauté until tender.
2. Add **three 14½-oz. cans of chicken stock** and **1½ lbs. of carrots,** peeled and thinly sliced. Simmer about 20 minutes, until carrots are tender.
3. Purée soup in a blender or food processor and return to the saucepan. Add **½ C. milk, juice of 1 lime, a pinch of curry powder** and **salt and pepper to taste.**
4. Serve chilled or warm, topped with a **dollop of plain yogurt** and **a sprinkle of chopped chives or parsley.**

Carrot Ginger Soup

SHOPPING LIST

PRODUCE	onion (1/2 medium)
	fresh ginger (1 medium piece, or 2 T. precrushed)
	garlic (1 clove, or 1/2 t. precrushed)
	carrots (1 1/2 lbs.)
	lime (1)
	chives or parsley (1 bunch) for garnish (optional)
DAIRY	unsalted butter (3 T. or 3/8 stick)
	milk (1/2 C.)
	plain yogurt (8-oz. carton) for garnish (optional)
CANNED ITEMS	chicken stock (three 14 1/2-oz. cans)
SEASONINGS	curry powder (pinch)
	salt and pepper (to taste)

Soups

POTATO, LEEK & CORN SOUP
Yields 4 servings

your preparation time: *5–10 minutes*

total time until ready: *40 minutes*

This is a very simple recipe. Most of the time required is for simmering the potatoes.

1. In a large saucepan, heat **3 T. olive oil** and sauté **2 medium washed and chopped leeks (white part only)** and **2 minced or pressed cloves of garlic (or 1 t. precrushed)**. Cook and stir for 5 minutes.
2. Add **three 14½-oz. cans of chicken stock** and **three large peeled and diced russet potatoes.** Bring to a boil. Simmer for 20 minutes, or until potatoes are tender.
3. Purée the soup in a blender or food processor and return it to the saucepan. Add **2 C. milk** and **2 C. frozen corn**. Heat until warm. Season with **salt and pepper to taste**.
4. Serve hot or cold, garnished with **chopped green onions, chives, parsley** or **dried tarragon**.

Potato, Leek & Corn Soup

SHOPPING LIST

PRODUCE	leeks (2 medium)
	garlic (2 cloves, or 1 t. precrushed)
	russet potatoes (3 large)
	green onions, chives or parsley (1 bunch) for garnish (optional)
DAIRY	milk (2 C.)
CANNED ITEMS	chicken stock (three 14 1/2-oz. cans)
SEASONINGS	salt and pepper (to taste)
	dried tarragon (to taste) for garnish (optional)
FROZEN ITEMS	frozen corn (2 C. or 10-oz. package)
MISC. ITEMS	olive oil (3 T.)

SALADS

Salads

WARM SPINACH SALAD & BAKED GOAT CHEESE WITH SHALLOT VINAIGRETTE

Yields 4-6 servings

your preparation time: *10–15 minutes*

total time until ready: *15–20 minutes*

---

1. *Dressing:* In a small saucepan, heat **2 T. olive oil** and sauté **3 minced shallots** and **2 minced or pressed cloves of garlic (or 1 t. precrushed)** until tender. Add **2 T. balsamic vinegar** and **2 T. Dijon mustard**. Slowly whisk in **½ C. extra virgin olive oil, a pinch of sugar** and **salt and pepper to taste**. Set aside and keep warm.
2. Preheat broiler for cheese.
3. Wash, stem and dry **2 bunches of spinach** and tear into bite-size pieces. Place in a large bowl.
4. Cut a **6-oz. log of goat cheese** into 6 rounds. Place the rounds in a shallow baking dish and drizzle with **olive oil** and sprinkle with **dried oregano, dried basil** and **salt and pepper**. Put dish in broiler and broil about 2–3 minutes, until tops are golden brown.
5. Toss spinach with warm vinaigrette. Arrange on individual plates topped with one slice of goat cheese and serve with a sliced **French baguette**.

Warm Spinach Salad & Goat Cheese

SHOPPING LIST

PRODUCE	shallots (3)
	garlic (2 cloves, or 1 t. precrushed)
	spinach (2 bunches)*
DAIRY	goat cheese (6-oz. log)
SEASONINGS	sugar (pinch)
	salt and pepper (to taste)
	dried oregano, dried basil (to taste)
MISC. ITEMS	balsamic vinegar (2 T.)
	Dijon mustard (2 T.)
	extra virgin olive oil (2 T. + 1/2 C.)
	French baguette (on the side)

Buy prewashed and prepared spinach leaves (two 10-oz. packages) to save time.

CLASSIC CAESAR SALAD

Yields 4 servings

your preparation time: *15 minutes*

total time until ready: *15 minutes*

---

1. *Dressing (makes enough for two batches):* Whisk together **2 minced or pressed cloves of garlic (or 1 t. precrushed), 5 rinsed and dried anchovy fillets crushed into a paste** (optional), **2 T. wine vinegar, juice of 2 lemons, 1/2 C. olive oil, a dash of Worcestershire sauce,** and **salt and pepper to taste**. *If you want a subtle garlic taste and have time, place 2–3 garlic cloves cut in half in 1/2 C. olive oil and let stand 1 hour or longer before preparing salad. Remove garlic and mix oil with other ingredients.*
2. Wash and dry **1 head of romaine lettuce**. Break into large pieces and place in a salad bowl.
3. Coddle **1 egg** by placing it in simmering (not boiling) water for 2 minutes.
4. Add egg, dressing, **1/2 C. grated Parmesan cheese** and **1 1/2 C. croutons** to the lettuce. Gently toss and serve with **freshly ground black pepper.**

SHOPPING LIST

PRODUCE	garlic (2 cloves, or 1 t. precrushed)
	lemons (2)
	romaine lettuce (1 medium head)*
DAIRY	egg (1)
	grated Parmesan cheese ($1/2$ C.)
MEAT/FISH	anchovy fillets (2-oz. can) (optional)
SEASONINGS	salt and pepper (to taste)
	Worcestershire sauce (dash)
MISC. ITEMS	wine vinegar (2 T.)
	olive oil ($1/2$ C.)
	croutons ($1 1/2$ C.)

Buy prewashed and prepared romaine lettuce to save time.

ORANGE-ALMOND SALAD WITH SESAME VINAIGRETTE

Yields 4 servings

your preparation time: *10 minutes*

total time until ready: *15–20 minutes*

---

1. *Dressing:* In a small bowl, whisk together **3 T. rice wine vinegar, 1 T. sugar, 3 T. light soy sauce, ½ t. dry mustard, 2 T. sesame oil, 1 T. toasted sesame seeds** and **½ C. peanut (or vegetable) oil.**
2. Wash and trim **½ head of red leaf lettuce** and **½ head of romaine lettuce**. Tear into bite-size pieces and mix in a large bowl.
3. Place lettuce on individual plates and top each with a quarter of the **11-oz. can of mandarin orange sections.**
4. Pour dressing on top of each serving and sprinkle each salad with a quarter of the **chopped green onion (1 stalk)** and **½ C. toasted slivered almonds.**

Orange-Almond Salad

SHOPPING LIST

PRODUCE	red leaf lettuce (1/2 head)
	romaine lettuce (1/2 head)
	green onion (1 stalk)
CANNED ITEMS	mandarin orange sections (11-oz. can)
SEASONINGS	sugar (1 T.)
	dry mustard (1/2 t.)
SPECIALTY/	rice wine vinegar (3 T.)
ETHNIC ITEMS	light soy sauce (3 T.)
	sesame oil (2 T.)
	toasted sesame seeds (1 T.)
MISC. ITEMS	peanut (or vegetable) oil (1/2 C.)
	toasted slivered almonds (1/2 C.)

Salads

FRESH TOMATOES, FARFALLE & FETA SALAD
Yields 4 servings

your preparation time: *15 minutes*

total time until ready: *30 minutes*

---

1. Prepare **½ lb. farfalle (bowtie) or other pasta** in boiling water until al dente (see package instructions). Rinse with cold water to cool pasta. Drain well.
2. In a large bowl, mix **2 chopped medium-size tomatoes, ½, peeled, seeded, halved and sliced cucumber, ½ peeled, seeded and chopped red or yellow bell pepper** (fresh or roasted—*see Tricolor Roasted Peppers on page 10 for roasting directions*), **4 T. balsamic vinegar** and **2 T. extra virgin olive oil**. If available, add approximately **10 chopped fresh basil** leaves and **2–3 t. capers**.
3. Toss pasta and vegetables together with **4 oz. crumbled feta cheese. Salt and pepper to taste.**
4. Serve cool or at room temperature with a **sliced French baguette**.

   This dish can also be served as a light main course for 2.

Fresh Tomatoes, Farfalle & Feta Salad

SHOPPING LIST

PRODUCE	tomatoes (2 medium)
	cucumber (1/2 medium)
	red or yellow bell pepper (1/2 medium)
	fresh basil (1 bunch) (optional)
DAIRY	feta cheese (4 oz.)
DRY ITEMS	farfalle (bowtie) or other pasta (1/2 lb.)
SEASONINGS	salt and pepper (to taste)
SPECIALTY/ ETHNIC ITEMS	capers (2–3 t.) (optional)
MISC. ITEMS	balsamic vinegar (4 T.)
	extra virgin olive oil (2 T.)
	French baguette (on the side)

MAIN DISHES

POULTRY/MEAT

SEAFOOD/PASTA

Main Dishes/Poultry

STIR-FRIED CHICKEN WITH BROCCOLI & CASHEWS

Yields 4 servings

your preparation time: *15 minutes*

total time until ready: *25–30 minutes*

---

1. Cut stems off **1¼ lbs. broccoli.** Cut flowerets into bite-size pieces.
2. Cut **1½ lbs. boneless, skinless chicken breasts** into bite-size pieces and mix in a bowl with the following ingredients: **1 t. grated fresh gingerroot (or 1 t. precrushed), ½ t. sugar, 2 T. light soy sauce, 1 T. oyster sauce, ½ t. crushed red pepper flakes** and **1 t. sesame oil.** Set aside.
3. Heat **1 T. peanut oil** in a wok or large skillet and sauté **1 minced or pressed garlic clove (or ½ t. precrushed)** for 20 seconds. Then add chicken and stir-fry over high heat until lightly browned. Do not overcook! Remove and return to bowl.
4. Add **1 T. peanut oil** and stir-fry broccoli for 2 minutes over high heat. Add **14½-oz. can of chicken stock** and return chicken to wok or skillet.
5. Mix **2–3 T. cornstarch** with **¼ C. water.** Stir into stock and cook until it thickens. Adjust seasonings–add a dash of soy sauce or oyster sauce if needed.
6. Add **½ C. unsalted cashews** and serve immediately.

Stir-Fried Chicken with Broccoli

SHOPPING LIST

PRODUCE	broccoli (1 1/4 lbs.)
	fresh gingerroot (1 small piece, or 1 t. precrushed)
	garlic (1 clove, or 1/2 t. precrushed)
MEAT/FISH	boneless, skinless chicken breasts (1 1/2 lbs.)
CANNED ITEMS	chicken stock (14 1/2-oz. can)
SEASONINGS	sugar (1/2 t.)
	crushed red pepper flakes (1/2 t.)
SPECIALTY/ ETHNIC ITEMS	light soy sauce (2 T.)
	oyster sauce (1 T.)
	sesame oil (1 t.)
MISC. ITEMS	peanut oil (2 T.)
	cornstarch (2–3 T.)
	unsalted cashews (1/2 C.)

Main Dishes/Poultry

FRESH ROSEMARY CHICKEN WITH WALNUTS
Yields 4-6 servings

your preparation time: *10 minutes*

total time until ready: *30–35 minutes*

---

1. In a shallow bowl, mix **1/4 C. flour**, **1/2 t. salt** and **1/4 t. pepper**. Dredge **6 boneless, skinless chicken breast halves** in flour mixture.
2. In a large skillet, heat **3 T. olive oil** over medium heat. Add chicken and sauté until lightly browned (about 3 minutes per side). Remove chicken from pan and cover. Reduce heat to medium.
3. Sauté **1/2 C. chopped walnuts** with remaining oil in pan until toasted. Remove from pan and keep on side.
4. Add **1 T. olive oil** to pan and sauté **1 minced or pressed garlic clove (or 1/2 t. precrushed)**, **1 1/2 T. fresh minced rosemary (or 1 T. dried)** and **1 T. dried thyme** for 2 minutes.
5. Stir in **2 C. red wine**, **14 1/2-oz. can of chicken stock** and **1/4 C. balsamic vinegar**. Simmer and stir occasionally for 10 minutes until sauce thickens. Return chicken to pan and simmer for 10 minutes.
6. Sprinkle **4 oz. crumbled feta cheese** over chicken.
7. Serve chicken breasts sprinkled with **toasted chopped walnuts** and **chopped chives**.

Fresh Rosemary Chicken with Walnuts

SHOPPING LIST

PRODUCE	garlic (1 clove, or 1/2 t. precrushed)
	fresh rosemary (1 1/2 T.)*
	chives (1 bunch) for garnish
DAIRY	feta cheese (4 oz.)
MEAT/FISH	boneless, skinless chicken breast halves (6)
CANNED ITEMS	chicken stock (14 1/2-oz. can)
SEASONINGS	salt (1/2 t.)
	pepper (1/4 t.)
	dried thyme (1 T.)
MISC. ITEMS	flour (1/4 C.)
	chopped walnuts (1/2 C.)
	olive oil (4 T.)
	red wine (2 C.)
	balsamic vinegar (1/4 C.)

If not available substitute dried rosemary (1 T.).

Main Dishes/Poultry

SHREDDED CHICKEN TACOS
Yields 4 servings

your preparation time: *15 minutes*

total time until ready: *35–40 minutes*

---

1. In a medium saucepan, heat **½ onion** and **6 C. water** to a boil. Add **6 boneless chicken breast halves** and skim off any foam that rises while they simmer. Add **½ t. dried thyme, 1 t. dried parsley, ½ t. dried marjoram** and **2 bay leaves**. Cover partially and simmer for 10 minutes, or until chicken juices run clear when pierced.
2. While chicken simmers, prepare vegetables: dice **½ onion** and mince or press **2 cloves of garlic (or use 1 t. pre-crushed)**. Chop **2 green onion stalks**. Stem, seed and finely chop **2–3 serrano chilies**.
3. Remove chicken and reserve broth. Let both cool.
4. Heat **1 T. olive oil** in a large skillet over medium-high heat. Sauté onion and garlic until lightly browned.
5. Reduce heat to medium and add a **well-drained 28-oz. can of whole tomatoes, green onions** and **chilies** and cook about 5 minutes. Crush tomatoes with a spoon as they cook.
6. Stir in **⅔ C. of reserved broth** and simmer 5–10 minutes. Add chicken and season with **salt and pepper**.
7. Serve with heated **corn tortillas, salsa** and **grated cheese**.

Shredded Chicken Tacos

SHOPPING LIST

PRODUCE	onion (1 medium)
	garlic (2 cloves, or 1 t. precrushed)
	green onions (2 stalks)
	serrano chilies (2–3)
DAIRY	grated Monterey Jack cheese (on the side)
MEAT/FISH	boneless chicken breast halves (6)
CANNED ITEMS	whole tomatoes (28-oz. can)
SEASONINGS	dried thyme (1/2 t.)
	dried parsley (1 t.)
	dried marjoram (1/2 t.)
	bay leaves (2)
	salt and pepper (to taste)
SPECIALTY/ ETHNIC ITEMS	corn tortillas (12)
	fresh salsa (16-oz. container)
MISC. ITEMS	olive oil (1 T.)

GRILLED SALAD WITH GOAT CHEESE FILLED CHICKEN

Yields 4 servings

your preparation time: *15 minutes*

total time until ready: *35 minutes*

---

1. Preheat grill or broiler.
2. Take **4 boneless chicken breast halves with skin attached** and separate a pocket between the skin and meat. Insert **1-2 oz. of goat cheese** inside each pocket. Rub chicken skin with **olive oil** and season with **salt and pepper**.
3. Wash **1 yellow and 1 red bell pepper, 1 eggplant, 2 zucchini** and **12 mushrooms**. Slice eggplant and zucchini into 1/4" thick rounds. Skewer zucchini slices and mushrooms on **bamboo skewers**. Brush all vegetables with olive oil. Slice **1 red onion** into 1/4" thick rounds.
4. Wash, dry, tear and mix **1 head of red leaf lettuce, 1 head of Boston or butterhead lettuce** and **2 bunches of arugula**.
5. *Vinaigrette:* Mix **2 T. Dijon mustard, 6 T. balsamic vinegar** and **1 minced shallot**, and whisk in **3/4 C. olive oil**. Season with **salt, pepper** and **1/2 t. sugar**.
6. Grill or broil chicken, skin side to the fire first, until browned (approximately 5 minutes per side). Place all the vegetables on the grill or broiler and cook until tender.
7. Peel and slice peppers. Then arrange vegetables and chicken on top of mixed greens. Serve with vinaigrette.

Grilled Salad with Chicken

SHOPPING LIST

PRODUCE	yellow bell pepper (1 medium)
	red bell pepper (1 medium)
	eggplant (1 small)
	zucchini (2 medium)
	mushrooms (12 medium)
	red onion (1 medium)
	red leaf lettuce (1 head)
	Boston or butterhead lettuce (1 head)
	arugula (2 bunches)
	shallot (1)
DAIRY	goat cheese (6-oz. log)
MEAT/FISH	boneless chicken breast halves with skin attached (4)
SEASONINGS	salt and pepper (to taste)
	sugar ($1/2$ t.)
MISC. ITEMS	bamboo skewers
	olive oil (1 C.)
	Dijon mustard (2 T.)
	balsamic vinegar (6 T.)

PARSLEY, SAGE, ROSEMARY & THYME CHICKEN AND GRAVY

Yields 4 servings

your preparation time: *5–10 minutes*

total time until ready: *15–20 minutes*

---

1. Cut **4 boneless, skinless chicken breast halves** into large bite-size chunks.
2. In a shallow bowl, mix **½ C. flour, ½ t. salt** and **½ t. pepper**. Dredge the chicken in the flour mixture.
3. Heat **3 T. olive oil** in a large skillet. Cook the chicken pieces until golden brown.
4. Add **one and a half 14½-oz. cans of chicken stock**. Let chicken cook 5 minutes longer.
5. Add **½ t. dried rosemary, ⅛ t. ground sage, 1 t. dried parsley** and **½ t. dried thyme**.
6. Mix **2-3 T. flour** with **remaining half can of chicken stock**. Add to chicken mixture to thicken gravy.
7. Cook until gravy thickens. Serve immediately over **rice** or **mashed potatoes.**

SHOPPING LIST

MEAT/FISH	boneless, skinless chicken breast halves (4)
CANNED ITEMS	chicken stock (two 14 1/2-oz. cans)
SEASONINGS	salt (1/2 t.) pepper (1/2 t.) dried rosemary (1/2 t.) ground sage (1/8 t.) dried parsley (1 t.) dried thyme (1/2 t.)
MISC. ITEMS	flour (1/2 C. + 2–3 T.) olive oil (3 T.) rice or mashed potatoes

Main Dishes/Meat

SESAME FLANK STEAK (WITH SPICY SESAME SAUCE)

Yields 4-6 servings

your preparation time: *10–15 minutes*

total time until ready: *25–30 minutes*

---

1. Preheat grill or broiler.
2. *Prepare marinade:* Mix **1/4 C. light soy sauce, 1/4 C. sesame oil, 1 minced or pressed garlic clove (or 1/2 t. precrushed) and 2 T. grated fresh gingerroot (or 2 T. precrushed)**. Rub the marinade on a **1 1/2-lb. flank steak**. You can cook it immediately or let the steak marinate for a while. *The longer it marinates, the more flavor the steak will have.*
3. If desired, prepare the Spicy Sesame Sauce on page 8 to serve with the flank steak.
4. Grill or broil steak 6" from the heat for 5–7 minutes per side.
5. Cut the steak diagonally into thin slices across the grain of the meat. Arrange on a platter, spoon juice from the steak on top, and serve with the Spicy Sesame Sauce.

SHOPPING LIST

PRODUCE	garlic (1 clove, or 1/2 t. precrushed) (add another 2 cloves or 1 t. precrushed if making sauce)
	fresh gingerroot (1 medium piece, or 2 T. precrushed)
	green onion (1 stalk, if making sauce)
MEAT/FISH	flank steak (1 1/2 lb.)
CANNED ITEMS	chicken stock (1 C. or half a 14 1/2-oz. can, if making sauce)
SEASONINGS	crushed red pepper flakes (1/2 t., if making sauce)
SPECIALTY/ ETHNIC ITEMS	light soy sauce (1/4 C.) (add additional 1/4 C. if making sauce)
	sesame oil (1/4 C.) (add 1 t. also if making sauce)
	toasted sesame seeds (2 T., if making sauce)

Main Dishes/Meat

BEEF WITH ASPARAGUS
Yields 4 servings

your preparation time: *15 minutes*

total time until ready: *25–30 minutes*

---

1. Slice **1 lb. boneless sirloin steak** or **flank steak** in thin strips across the grain.
2. *Marinade:* Combine **1 t. salt, 1 t. sugar, 1 T. white wine, 1 t. light soy sauce, 1 T. oyster sauce** and **1 T. cornstarch**. Combine marinade and steak together.
3. Remove tough ends of **1½ lbs. asparagus**. Cut spears into ½" diagonal slices.
4. Heat **2 T. peanut oil** in a wok or large skillet. Add beef and stir-fry for 2 minutes over high heat. Remove from wok and set aside.
5. Heat **1 T. peanut oil** in wok or skillet and add **1 minced or pressed garlic clove (or ½ t. precrushed)** and **1 t. crushed red pepper flakes**. Stir-fry for 20 seconds. Then add asparagus and stir-fry for 2 minutes.
6. **Add 1 T. oyster sauce, ½ t. salt, ½ t. sugar** and **14½-oz. can of chicken stock**. Cook, uncovered, for 2 minutes. Add beef and stir.
7. Mix **2–3 T. cornstarch** with **¼ C. water** and **1 T. sesame oil**. Stir into broth and cook until sauce is thick.

Beef with Asparagus

SHOPPING LIST

PRODUCE	asparagus (1½ lbs.)
	garlic (1 clove, or ½ t. precrushed)
MEAT/FISH	boneless sirloin steak or flank steak (1 lb.)
CANNED ITEMS	chicken stock (14½-oz. can)
SEASONINGS	salt (1½ t.)
	sugar (1½ t.)
	crushed red pepper flakes (1 t.)
SPECIALTY/ETHNIC ITEMS	light soy sauce (1 t.)
	oyster sauce (2 T.)
	sesame oil (1 T.)
MISC. ITEMS	white wine (1 T.)
	cornstarch (3–4 T.)
	peanut oil (3 T.)

Main Dishes/Meat

COLORFUL TERIYAKI KEBABS
Yields 4 servings

your preparation time: *15–20 minutes*

total time until ready: *25–30 minutes*

---

1. Preheat grill or broiler.
2. *Marinade.* In a bowl, whisk **3 T. peanut oil, 1/2 C. light soy sauce, 1/4 C. rice wine vinegar, 1 minced green onion stalk, 1 minced or pressed garlic clove (or 1/2 t. precrushed), 1 t. grated fresh gingerroot (or 1 t. precrushed) and 2 T. sugar.** Cut **1 1/2 lbs. boneless sirloin steak** into 1" to 1 1/2" squares and combine with marinade. Set aside.
3. Trim and seed **1 yellow or red bell pepper**. Cut it into 1" to 1 1/2" pieces. Wash and trim **12 mushrooms**. Wash **1 medium zucchini** and slice it into 12 rounds. Cut **1/2 purple onion** into quarters and separate layers. Wash **12 cherry tomatoes**. Open and drain **8-oz. can of pineapple chunks** (or use fresh pineapple if available).
4. Skewer all ingredients on **12 bamboo or metal skewers**. Divide ingredients evenly among 12 skewers and alternate items to create a colorful mix. Reserve marinade.
5. Grill on medium-hot coals or broil for 8–10 minutes, turning every 2–3 minutes. Brush skewers with marinade as they cook.

Colorful Teriyaki Kebabs

SHOPPING LIST

PRODUCE	green onion (1 stalk)
	garlic (1 clove, or 1/2 t. precrushed)
	fresh gingerroot (1 small piece, or 1 t. precrushed)
	yellow or red bell pepper (1 medium)
	mushrooms (12 medium)
	zucchini (1 medium)
	purple onion (1/2 medium)
	cherry tomatoes (12)
MEAT/FISH	boneless sirloin steak (1 1/2 lbs.)
CANNED ITEMS	pineapple chunks (8-oz. can)
	or fresh pineapple if available
SEASONINGS	sugar (2 T.)
SPECIALTY/	light soy sauce (1/2 C.)
ETHNIC ITEMS	rice wine vinegar (1/4 C.)
MISC. ITEMS	peanut oil (3 T.)
	bamboo or metal skewers (12)

Main Dishes/Meat

MUSTARD PORK CHOPS WITH COUSCOUS
Yields 4 servings

your preparation time: *10 minutes*

total time until ready: *25 minutes*

---

1. Preheat broiler.
2. Whisk **4 T. Dijon mustard, juice of 1 lime** and **2 t. ground cumin** in a small bowl.
3. In a medium saucepan, combine a **14½-oz. can of chicken stock, 1 T. butter** and **2 t. dried thyme,** and heat until it boils. Add **1 C. couscous** and remove from heat. Allow to stand (until water is absorbed).
4. Arrange **8-12 thin boneless pork chops** on a foil-lined broiler pan. Spread top of chops with half of mustard mixture. Sprinkle with **bread crumbs** or *panko.*
5. Broil chops 2" from the heat for 5–6 minutes. Turn chops over and spread other half of mustard mixture and sprinkle with bread crumbs. Broil for 5 minutes more.
6. Serve immediately with couscous.

Mustard Pork Chops with Couscous

SHOPPING LIST

PRODUCE	lime (1 medium)
DAIRY	butter (1 T. or 1/8 stick)
MEAT/FISH	thin, boneless pork chops (8–12)
CANNED ITEMS	chicken stock (14 1/2-oz. can)
SEASONINGS	ground cumin (2 t.) dried thyme (2 t.)
SPECIALTY/ ETHNIC ITEMS	couscous (1 C.)
MISC. ITEMS	Dijon mustard (4 T.) bread crumbs (3/4–1 C.) or (if available) *panko* (Japanese bread crumbs) is best. It can be found in specialty shops or the Oriental section of supermarkets.

GRILLED HALIBUT WITH BASIL–PINE NUT BUTTER

Yields 4 servings

your preparation time: *15 minutes*

total time until ready: *30 minutes*

---

1. Preheat grill or broiler.
2. Rub **1 T. olive oil** on **1½ lbs. halibut steak**. Squeeze **juice of 1 lime** on top and set aside.
3. *Basil–Pine Nut Butter:* In a small bowl, with a fork (or in a blender), mix **4 T. softened butter, 1 t. lemon juice, 3 T. toasted and chopped pine nuts, 1 T. fresh minced basil** and **salt and pepper to taste**. Roll butter into a log shape and wrap in waxed paper or plastic. Chill.
4. Place halibut on hot coals or in broiler. Grill or broil for 3 minutes per side, or until fish turns opaque.
5. Top individual portions of halibut with a slice of the Basil–Pine Nut Butter. Serve immediately.

Grilled Halibut & Basil–Pine Nut Butter

SHOPPING LIST

PRODUCE	lime (1 medium)
	lemon (1 medium)
	basil (1 bunch)
DAIRY	butter (4 T. or 1/2 stick)
MEAT/FISH	halibut steak (1 1/2 lbs.)
SEASONINGS	salt and pepper (to taste)
MISC. ITEMS	olive oil (1 T.)
	toasted pine nuts (3 T.)

SALMON, FRESH TOMATOES & SPAGHETTINI

Yields 4 servings

your preparation time: *15–20 minutes*

total time until ready: *25–30 minutes*

---

1. Preheat grill or broiler. Bring a large pot of water to boil for pasta.
2. In a medium bowl, mix **3 C. chopped tomatoes, 1/2 C. olive oil, 1/2 C. chopped fresh basil, 1 finely chopped shallot, 1/4 C. balsamic vinegar, 1 minced green onion stalk, 1 t. lemon zest, 1/2 t. salt, 1 t. black pepper, a pinch of cayenne pepper** and **1/2 C. red wine**. Set aside at room temperature.
3. Cook **1 lb. spaghettini** according to package directions. Drain and toss with **2 T. olive oil**.
4. While pasta is cooking, squeeze **juice of 1 lemon** on a **1 1/2-lb. salmon fillet.** Then **salt and pepper to taste**. Broil or grill salmon until opaque, about 4–5 minutes per side.
5. Divide pasta among 4 plates. Place a quarter of the salmon fillet on each plate and spoon tomato mixture over salmon and pasta. Sprinkle each with **1–2 T. grated Parmesan cheese** and serve immediately.

Salmon, Fresh Tomatoes & Spaghettini

SHOPPING LIST

PRODUCE	tomatoes (3–4 medium)
	fresh basil (1 bunch)
	shallot (1)
	green onion (1 stalk)
	lemon (1)
DAIRY	grated Parmesan cheese (4–8 T.)
MEAT/FISH	salmon fillet (1 1/2 lb.)
DRIED FOODS	spaghettini (or angel hair pasta) (1 lb.)
SEASONINGS	salt (1/2 t. and to taste)
	pepper (1 t. and to taste)
	cayenne pepper (pinch)
MISC. ITEMS	olive oil (1/2 C. + 2 T.)
	balsamic vinegar (1/4 C.)
	red wine (1/2 C.)

Main Dishes/Seafood

QUICK GARLIC SHRIMP
Yields 4 servings

your preparation time: *10 minutes*

total time until ready: *15 minutes*

---

1. Shell and devein **1 lb. large shrimp**.
2. Mix **4½ t. cornstarch, 2 T. light soy sauce, 2 T. rice wine vinegar or dry sherry** and **½ C. chicken stock.** Set aside.
3. Heat **1 T. olive oil** in a wok or large skillet.
4. Add **2–3 minced or pressed garlic cloves (or 1 to 1½ t. precrushed)** and stir-fry quickly for 10–20 seconds.
5. Add shrimp and **juice of 1 lemon**. Stir-fry until shrimp turns pink. Do not overcook!
6. Stir in **2 chopped green onion stalks**. Add cornstarch mixture and cook until sauce *just* thickens. Do not overcook! Serve immediately.

Quick Garlic Shrimp

SHOPPING LIST

PRODUCE	garlic (2–3 cloves, or 1 to 1 1/2 t. precrushed)
	lemon (1 medium)
	green onion (2 stalks)
MEAT/FISH	large shrimp (1 lb.)
CANNED ITEMS	chicken stock (1/2 C. or a quarter of a 14 1/2-oz. can)
SPECIALTY/ ETHNIC ITEMS	light soy sauce (2 T.)
	rice wine vinegar or dry sherry (2 T.)
MISC. ITEMS	cornstarch (4 1/2 t.)
	olive oil (1 T.)

Main Dishes/Seafood

BASIL & LEMON STUFFED TROUT
Yields 4 servings

your preparation time: *10 minutes*

total time until ready: *20–30 minutes*

---

1. Preheat grill or broiler.
2. Clean **4 fresh whole trout (10–12 oz. each) with head and tail still on**. Open the trout and remove any small bones with **tweezers.** Brush the inside and outside of each trout with **olive oil, a squeeze of lemon juice,** and a **sprinkle of salt and pepper**.
3. Place **3–4 lemon slices** and **5–6 basil leaves** in each fish.
4. Grill fish on medium-hot coals or broil for approximately 5 minutes per side, or until flesh is white and opaque. Avoid damaging skin by carefully turning fish.
5. Serve with **salad** and a **French baguette**.

Basil & Lemon Stuffed Trout

SHOPPING LIST

PRODUCE	lemon (3 medium)
	fresh basil (1 bunch)
MEAT/FISH	fresh (not frozen) whole trout (4) (10–12 oz. each)
SEASONINGS	salt and pepper (to taste)
MISC. ITEMS	olive oil (to brush on fish)
	tweezers (to remove bones from trout)
	salad (on the side)
	French baguette (on the side)

SPICY THAI SWORDFISH
Yields 4 servings

your preparation time: 5–10 minutes

total time until ready: 30 minutes

---

1. Preheat grill or broiler.
2. *Marinade:* In small glass bowl, mix **1/2 C. rice wine vinegar (or distilled white vinegar), juice of 1/2 lemon, 1/4 C. olive oil, 2 seeded and sliced green serrano chilies, 1/2 t. crushed red pepper flakes, 1 t. lemon zest, 1/4 t. cayenne pepper** and **1/2 t. chili powder**.
3. Place **four 1/2-lb. (1" thick) swordfish steaks** in a shallow glass pan. Pour marinade on top. Let fish marinate for 15–30 minutes (depending on how much time you have).
4. Grill over hot coals or broil swordfish approximately 4–5 minutes per side. Serve immediately.

Spicy Thai Swordfish

SHOPPING LIST

PRODUCE	lemon (1 medium)
	serrano chilies (2)
MEAT/FISH	swordfish steaks (four 1/2-lb, 1" thick steaks)
SEASONINGS	crushed red pepper flakes (1/2 t.)
	cayenne pepper (1/4 t.)
	chili powder (1/2 t.)
SPECIALTY/ ETHNIC ITEMS	rice wine vinegar (or distilled white vinegar) (1/2 C.)
MISC. ITEMS	olive oil (1/4 C.)

Main Dishes/Pasta

AGNOLOTTI, ZUCCHINI & HERBS

Yields 2 servings

your preparation time: 5 minutes

total time until ready: 20–30 minutes

---

1. Slice **3 medium zucchini** into thin rounds.
2. Cook a **9-oz. package of fresh porcini mushroom–stuffed agnolotti (or other fresh stuffed pasta)** according to package directions. Do not overcook!
3. Heat **2 T. olive oil** with **2 minced or pressed garlic cloves (or 1 t. precrushed)** until garlic releases aroma. Sauté zucchini for 30 seconds. Add **juice of ½ lemon, 1 t. dried thyme leaves, ½ t. ground sage, 1 t. dried basil, ¼ t. fennel seeds** and **salt and pepper to taste**. Sauté until zucchini is tender yet crunchy.
4. Add agnolotti and mix well. If the pasta and zucchini seem dry add **¼ C. water** (the moisture of the dish depends on how much water the zucchini releases). Adjust seasonings to taste. Toss with **¼ C. grated Parmesan cheese**.
5. Serve immediately with a **French baguette** on the side.

Agnolotti, Zucchini & Herbs

SHOPPING LIST

PRODUCE	zucchini (3 medium)
	garlic (2 cloves, or 1 t. precrushed)
	lemon (1/2 medium)
DAIRY	grated Parmesan cheese (1/4 C.)
DRIED BEANS/ PASTA/RICE	porcini mushroom–stuffed agnolotti or other fresh stuffed pasta (such as cheese-filled ravioli) (9-oz. package)
SEASONINGS	dried thyme leaves (1 t.)
	ground sage (1/2 t.)
	dried basil (1 t.)
	fennel seeds (1/4 t.)
	salt and pepper (to taste)
MISC. ITEMS	olive oil (2 T.)
	French baguette (on the side)

Main Dishes / Pasta

CHEESE RAVIOLI WITH ROASTED RED PEPPER SAUCE

Yields 4 servings

your preparation time: *15 minutes*

total time until ready: *30–40 minutes*

---

1. Bring a large pot of water to boil for the ravioli.
2. Roast **3–4 large red bell peppers** *(see Tricolor Peppers recipe on page 10).* Peel, seed and purée peppers in food processor or blender.
3. In a saucepan, heat **1 T. olive oil** and add **3 minced or pressed garlic cloves (or 1½ t. precrushed)**. Cook until garlic releases aroma; then add puréed peppers, **1 T. balsamic vinegar** and **½ C. chicken stock**. Add **chopped fresh or dried parsley, thyme** and/or **basil** to taste. **Salt and pepper to taste.**
4. Simmer sauce while preparing ravioli.
5. Cook **two 9-oz. packages of fresh ricotta-filled ravioli (or other pasta of choice)** according to package instructions.
6. Serve pasta with sauce and **fresh grated Parmesan cheese** on the side.

Cheese Ravioli with Roasted Pepper Sauce

SHOPPING LIST

PRODUCE	red bell peppers (3–4 large)
	garlic (3 cloves, or 1 1/2 t. precrushed)
	fresh parsley, thyme and/or basil*
	(to taste)
DAIRY	fresh grated Parmesan cheese (on the side)
DRIED BEANS/ PASTA/RICE	Fresh ricotta-filled ravioli or other fresh stuffed pasta (two 9-oz. pkgs.)
CANNED ITEMS	chicken stock (1/2 C. or a quarter of a 14 1/2-oz. can)
SEASONINGS	salt and pepper (to taste)
MISC. ITEMS	olive oil (1 T.)
	balsamic vinegar (1 T.)

Substitute dried seasonings (to taste) if fresh are not available.

Main Dishes/Pasta

PENNE À LA PUTTANESCA
Yields 4 servings

your preparation time: *5 minutes*

total time until ready: *25–30 minutes*

---

1. Begin heating a large pot of water for the pasta.
2. Drain **two 28-oz. cans of whole peeled Italian plum tomatoes**.
3. Heat **3 T. olive oil** in a skillet. Take a **2-oz. can of anchovy fillets** (optional); rinse, dry and chop them. Add anchovies and **4 minced or pressed garlic cloves (or 2 t. precrushed)** to skillet and mash into a paste. Cook for 30–45 seconds.
4. Add tomatoes and bring to a boil. Crush tomatoes with the back of a wooden spoon. Add **1 t. oregano, ¼ t. crushed red pepper flakes, ¼ C. drained capers, 1 C. coarsely chopped pitted black olives** and **½ C. chopped parsley**. Add **salt and pepper to taste**. Stir frequently.
5. Reduce heat to a simmer.
6. Cook **1 lb. penne** according to package directions.
7. Serve sauce over penne with **grated Parmesan cheese** on the side.

Penne à la Puttanesca

SHOPPING LIST

PRODUCE	garlic (4 cloves, or 2 t. precrushed)
	parsley (1 bunch)
DAIRY	grated Parmesan cheese (on the side)
DRIED BEANS/ PASTA/RICE	penne pasta (1 lb.)
CANNED ITEMS	whole peeled Italian plum tomatoes (two 28-oz. cans)
	anchovy fillets (2-oz. can) (optional)
	chopped pitted black olives (two 4 1/4-oz. cans)
SEASONINGS	oregano (1 t.)
	crushed red pepper flakes (1/4 t.)
	salt and pepper to taste
SPECIALTY/ ETHNIC ITEMS	capers (1/4 C. or half a 4-oz. jar)
MISC. ITEMS	olive oil (3 T.)

Main Dishes/Pasta

PESTO LINGUINE
Yields 4 servings

your preparation time: *10 minutes*

total time until ready: *20 minutes*

---

1. Begin heating water in a large pot for the linguine.
2. *Pesto Sauce:* Process **2 C. fresh basil leaves, 4 garlic cloves (or 2 t. precrushed)** and **1/4 C. toasted pine nuts** in a food processor until finely chopped. With machine running, add **1/4 C. olive oil** in a steady stream.
3. Turn off the machine and add **1/2 C. grated Parmesan cheese**. Process again until mixed. Add another **1/4 C. olive oil** while the machine is running. Turn off and add **salt and pepper to taste**.
4. Cook **1 lb. linguine** according to package instructions. Drain pasta and toss with pesto.
5. Serve immediately with **grated Parmesan cheese** on the side.

Pesto Linguine

SHOPPING LIST

PRODUCE	basil leaves (2 C., or 3–4 bunches)
	garlic (4 cloves, or 2 t. precrushed)
DAIRY	grated Parmesan cheese (on the side)
DRIED BEANS/ PASTA/RICE	linguine (1 lb.)
SEASONINGS	salt and pepper (to taste)
MISC. ITEMS	toasted pine nuts (1/4 C.)
	olive oil (1/2 C.)

SIMPLY DELICIOUS
DESSERTS

Desserts

ICE CREAM (OR FROZEN YOGURT) FILLED PUFFED PASTRY & RASPBERRY SAUCE

Yields 9 pastries

your preparation time: *10 minutes*

total time until ready: *20 minutes*

---

1. Preheat oven to 350°.
2. Cut **1 Pepperidge Farm Puff Pastry Sheet** with a large round cookie cutter or into 9 squares. Beat **1 egg yolk** and brush it on top of each pastry. Bake for 10 minutes until tops are golden.
3. Purée a **10-oz. package of fresh frozen (no sugar added) raspberries**. Add **sugar to taste** (¼ C. or less) and **fresh lemon juice to taste**. Strain.
4. Place a pool of raspberry sauce on a dessert plate.
5. After pastries are baked, tear apart top and bottom halves. Place a **scoop of vanilla ice cream** or **frozen yogurt** between the halves and sandwich them together.
6. Place pastry on top of raspberry sauce.
7. Garnish with **fresh raspberries** and **mint leaves**.

Ice Cream Filled Puff Pastry

SHOPPING LIST

PRODUCE	lemon (1 medium)
	fresh raspberries (for garnish)
	mint leaves (for garnish)
DAIRY	egg (1)
SEASONINGS	sugar ($1/4$ C.)
FROZEN ITEMS	Pepperidge Farm Puff Pastry Sheets (A $17 1/4$-oz. package contains 2 unbaked sheets.)
	fresh frozen (no sugar added) raspberries (10-oz. package)
	vanilla ice cream or frozen yogurt (1 pint)

APPLE BLACKBERRY WALNUT COBBLER
Yields 6 servings

your preparation time: *10–15 minutes*

total time until ready: *45–50 minutes*

This is a very simple dessert to make. Most of the time required is for baking.

1. Preheat oven to 350°.
2. Butter a 9 x 9" baking dish. Peel, core and thinly slice **4–5 McIntosh apples**. Place in prepared baking dish.
3. Top with a **16-oz. package of fresh frozen blackberries** (do not thaw). Sprinkle with **1/3 C. sugar**, **1/2 T. lemon juice** and **2 T. flour**.
4. In a small bowl, combine **1/2 C. rolled oats**, **1/2 C. flour**, **1/2 C. chopped walnuts**, **5 T. melted butter**, **1/2 C. brown sugar** and **1 t. cinnamon** until crumbly.
5. Sprinkle topping evenly over apples and blackberries. Bake approximately 35–40 minutes, until fruit is bubbly and topping is golden.
6. Serve with **vanilla frozen yogurt**.

Apple   Blackberry   Walnut   Cobbler

SHOPPING LIST

PRODUCE	McIntosh apples (4–5 medium)
	lemon (1 medium)
DAIRY	butter (5 T. or 5/8 stick)
BAKING ITEMS	sugar (1/3 C.)
	rolled oats (1/2 C.)
	flour (2 T. + 1/2 C.)
	chopped walnuts (1/2 C.)
	brown sugar (1/2 C.)
	ground cinnamon (1 t.)
FROZEN ITEMS	fresh frozen blackberries (16-oz. package)
	vanilla frozen yogurt (1 pint)

Desserts

TRIPLE CHOCOLATE WALNUT BROWNIES
Yields 4 servings

your preparation time: *10 minutes*

total time until ready: *35–40 minutes*

---

1. Preheat oven to 350°.
2. In a large microwavable bowl, microwave (or melt in a double boiler) **6 oz. chopped bittersweet chocolate, 2 oz. chopped unsweetened baking chocolate** and **1½ sticks of butter** until melted and mixture is smooth (approximately 2 minutes). *Do not overcook!*
3. Add **1½ C. sugar** and stir until blended.
4. Add **4 large eggs**, one at a time, mixing well after each egg.
5. Add **1½ t. vanilla extract**. Mix well.
6. Mix in **1 t. salt** and **1 C. all-purpose flour** until blended.
7. Add **1 C. coarsely chopped walnuts** and **1 C. semisweet chocolate chips**.
8. Spread batter in greased 9 x 13 x 2" baking pan. Bake for 25–30 minutes, or until a wooden pick inserted in the center comes out almost clean. *Do not overcook.*
9. Cool in pan and cut into 24 squares.

Triple Chocolate Walnut Brownies

SHOPPING LIST

DAIRY
butter (3/4 C. or 1 1/2 sticks)
eggs (4 large)

BAKING ITEMS
bittersweet chocolate (6 oz.)
unsweetened baking chocolate (2 oz.)
sugar (1 1/2 C.)
vanilla extract (1 1/2 t.)
salt (1 t.)
all-purpose flour (1 C.)
chopped walnuts (1 C.)
semisweet chocolate chips (1 C.)

Desserts

POACHED PEARS WITH MAPLE PECAN SAUCE
Yields 4 servings

your preparation time: *10 minutes*

total time until ready: *60 minutes*

This is a very simple recipe. Most of the time required is for poaching and cooling the pears, which can be done while dinner is being prepared and eaten.

1. Peel **4 large D'Anjou pears**, leaving stem intact. Cut a thin slice from the bottom so the pears sit upright.
2. In a medium saucepan, combine **6 C. water, 1/2 C. sugar, 1 cinnamon stick, 1 t. vanilla extract** and **juice of 1 lemon**. Bring to a boil. Lower heat, add pears and simmer until tender (30–45 minutes).
3. Let pears cool in liquid. Refrigerate or, if time is short, put pears in the freezer for 10–15 minutes.
4. In a small saucepan, cook **1 C. pure maple syrup** and **2 t. fresh lemon juice** over low heat until it reduces to 3/4 C. Add **1/3 C. chopped pecans** and keep warm.
5. Remove pears from liquid and put on individual dessert plates. Spoon hot sauce on top of each pear and serve immediately.

Poached Pears with Maple Pecan Sauce

SHOPPING LIST

PRODUCE	D'Anjou pears (4 large)
	lemon (1 medium)
BAKING ITEMS	sugar (1/2 C.)
	cinnamon stick (1)
	vanilla extract (1 t.)
	chopped pecans (1/3 C. or 2 oz.)
MISC. ITEMS	pure maple syrup (1 C.)

YOUR FAVORITE

RECIPE

INGREDIENTS

FAVORITE RECIPE INGREDIENTS

recipe name

yield

reference source/pg. no.

ingredients

recipe name

yield

reference source/pg. no.

ingredients

FAVORITE RECIPE INGREDIENTS

recipe name

yield

reference source/pg. no.

ingredients

recipe name

yield

reference source/pg. no.

ingredients

FAVORITE RECIPE INGREDIENTS

recipe name

yield

reference source/pg. no.

ingredients

---

recipe name

yield

reference source/pg. no.

ingredients

FAVORITE RECIPE INGREDIENTS

recipe name

yield

reference source/pg. no.

ingredients

recipe name

yield

reference source/pg. no.

ingredients

FAVORITE RECIPE INGREDIENTS

recipe name

yield

reference source/pg. no.

ingredients

---

recipe name

yield

reference source/pg. no.

ingredients

FAVORITE RECIPE INGREDIENTS

recipe name

yield

reference source/pg. no.

ingredients

recipe name

yield

reference source/pg. no.

ingredients

FAVORITE RECIPE INGREDIENTS

recipe name

yield

reference source/pg. no.

ingredients

recipe name

yield

reference source/pg. no.

ingredients

FAVORITE RECIPE INGREDIENTS

recipe name

yield

reference source/pg. no.

ingredients

recipe name

yield

reference source/pg. no.

ingredients

FAVORITE RECIPE INGREDIENTS

recipe name

yield

reference source/pg. no.

ingredients

---

recipe name

yield

reference source/pg. no.

ingredients

FAVORITE RECIPE INGREDIENTS

recipe name

yield

reference source/pg. no.

ingredients

recipe name

yield

reference source/pg. no.

ingredients

FAVORITE RECIPE INGREDIENTS

recipe name

yield

reference source/pg. no.

ingredients

recipe name

yield

reference source/pg. no.

ingredients